1985

To Rod:

a chairside view of some of the beauty we enjoyed while Kim was with you. A totem pole would be more representative souvenir but a little bulky to mail. Hope you & Carrie get the chance to see some of this country first hand some day.

With love & appreciation,

Mom & Dad

THE BEAUTY OF
CANADA

THE BEAUTY OF CANADA

Pat Pierce

DEANS
INTERNATIONAL
PUBLISHING

Dedication
In memory of Ruth and Lorne Culp

Acknowledgements

Every effort has been made to trace copyright holders. Further information would be gratefully received.

p. 9: From *The Collected Poems of Robert Service*. Used by permission, Estate of Robert W. Service (from *The Law of the Yukon*) © 1907 Dodd, Mead and Company.

p. 19 top: From *To the Wild Country* by John and Janet Foster, Van Nostrand Reinhold, 1975. Used by permission of the authors.

p. 19 bottom: From *Inutitut* Magazine, Summer/Fall, 1968. Used by permission of Indian and Northern Affairs Canada.

p. 25 top: From *Canada and the Canadians* by George Woodcock, Faber and Faber, London. Used by permission of the publishers.

p. 25 middle: From *Canada: Tomorrow's Giant* by Bruce Hutchison, Longman Canada, 1957.

p. 25 bottom: From *Hundreds and Thousands, The Journals of Emily Carr*, © 1966 Clarke, Irwin. (1983) Inc. Used by permission.

p. 43 top: From "Beyond the Horizon" by Miriam Waddington, published by *Weekend Magazine*, Montreal, May 11, 1974. Used by permission of the author.

p. 43 bottom: From *Equations of Love* by Ethel Wilson. Reprinted with the permission of the University of British Columbia Library.

p. 69 top: From *Maria Chapdelaine* by Louis Hémon. Used by permission of Macmillan of Canada.

p. 69 bottom: From *Two Solitudes* by Hugh MacLennan. Used by permission.

p. 113 top: From *Canada* by Kildaire Dobbs, Macmillan of Canada, 1964.

p. 113 bottom: From *This Rock Within the Sea* by Farley Mowat, McClelland and Stewart, Toronto; Little, Brown and Company, Boston; Pan Books, London. Used by permission.

Photographic acknowledgements

All photographs in this book are by Colour Library International, London, with the exception of the following:

Bruce Coleman, London, page 128 bottom; Daily Telegraph Colour Library, London, endpapers, title page, pages 18-19, 20 bottom, 21 top, 22, 29, 30, 31, 32-33, 37, 40, 42-43, 44, 48 top, 49, 50, 51, 53, 60, 62 bottom, 66-67, 71, 76, 78, 81, 89, 94-95, 100-101, 104, 106-107, 115, 116, 118, 119, 122, 123, 124, 125, 126, 127, 128 top; Michael Dent, London, pages 36, 41, 58 bottom, 61, 63, 66, 76-77, 77 bottom, 100, 105, 109, 110, 111, 112-113, 114-115, 116-117, 121; Zefa, London, page 20 top

Front cover: Jasper National Park (The Image Bank)
Back cover: Quebec City (Michael Dent)

Published by
Deans International Publishing
52-54 Southwark Street, London SE1 1UA
A division of The Hamlyn Publishing Group Limited
London · New York · Sydney · Toronto

Copyright © The Hamlyn Publishing Group Limited 1984, 1985
ISBN 0 600 39126 4

Printed in Italy

Contents

Introduction

Canada, a land of six time zones, is the second largest country in the world, with mountains, prairies, rugged coastlines pounded by three oceans, tundra and the polar ice cap. And the people who have met this great and challenging land head-on are a fascinating mix of cultures, with dozens of varied heritages. To all Canada was, and still is, a land of promise and hope. This belief has drawn people from all over the world, people who were willing to endure temporary hardship in order to achieve the dream they knew was attainable. So we have timeless villages, comfortable farming communities, fishing harbours, pleasant towns, industrial giants and cities to rival any in the world.

The North

There is another Canada, an immense land that holds tightly on to its many secrets. In the vastness of Canada's North, polar bears dig their snow dens, the aurora borealis swirls across the evening sky, and Eskimos teach their sons the ancient skills of survival. Each spring these seemingly empty lands are surprisingly and suddenly blanketed with colourful wildflowers rooted in the thin soil covering the permafrost. Here 100000 or more caribou gather during their annual migration.

Few people have seen, or are perhaps even aware of, the South Nahanni River, a tributary of the great Mackenzie River, which occupies one of the Earth's deepest canyon systems, the powerful Virginia Falls which are more than one and a half times the height of Niagara, and the vast treeless tundra. Canada's North, with its ice and wilderness has, since the beginning of time, set its own standards for those with whom it will share its secrets. Special people, unique people, have known and know this land. Today's citizens of the Northwest Territories and the Yukon understand that they have something of the courage and humour – the romance and drama – of those first people, the Inuit and the Indians. The Inuit, as the Eskimos of the polar region call themselves, and the Athabascan Indians, who live in the subarctic forested area of northern wilderness, once had the pulse of this land in their very being. Their descendants, after a period of tragic decline, are once more listening for that pulse.

At their peak the Inuit probably numbered around 65000, a population that was sparingly scattered over an area so vast, with an environment so harsh, that the existence of such a successful culture seems a cause for wonder. The only form of social organization was the family, and these small groups, of necessity eager to co-operate among themselves and with others, were extremely well-adapted to make the best of their meagre resources. The cold or the distances did not worry them particularly. If a storm blew up, the Inuit could quickly build an ice shelter, one of many ingenious adaptations in lifestyle and clothing. Their good humour did, however, overlay a constant worry – that of hunger. Many had starved in the past when the caribou did not come, or some other calamity struck. Legends, stories and carvings reflect their interest in the Hunt, and the animals which they respected. After a kill the animal's throat was slit or the head cut off to release its spirit. A salt-water animal was offered fresh water, the hunter hoping that its spirit would report back to Taleelayo, goddess of the sea and sea animals, on how well it had been treated; thus, it might allow itself to be captured again. The Athabascan Indians had a similar respect for other living things. For they too had life, equal to theirs and part of the whole. And the creature had given them life, for which it was thanked.

In this culture the oral tradition was strong, because no written language existed. There is a truly remarkable example of just how strong this tradition was. The world of the Inuit began to change dramatically with the arrival of the first explorers. The English navigator Martin Frobisher made three voyages to the Arctic in three successive years. During the second voyage in 1577, the Inuit, whose wily behaviour indicated that they had already had experience of white men, captured five of his sailors. Their fate remained a mystery until about 1862 when an American explorer, Charles F. Hall, visited the

Frobisher Bay area for two years, learning the language. From the old women he heard a reasonably accurate account of Frobisher's visits and of the fate of the men. Apparently they were released after a time and went to an island where they knew Frobisher had left some wood. There they built a boat, but they perished in the cold. Only then was the story completed – 300 years later.

The explorers, whalers, fur-traders and all the others who came to the North eventually left. Over-hunting, disease, alcohol and guns were too much for this delicately balanced culture to endure. By the turn of this century, one-third of the entire Canadian Inuit population had died. Today the descendants of the survivors of this formerly nomadic people live in scattered settlements throughout the Northwest Territories, in northern Quebec and Labrador. For example, some live around the shores of Hudson Bay. Wherever

they are, they hunt, trap and fish; some work as guides and park wardens or on construction projects, while others live on government assistance.

Their skill at carving dates far back in time to the ritual carvings and the decoration of the weapons and utensils of their predecessors – the people of the Dorset culture (600 BC–AD 1000) and the Thule culture which replaced it. An artist, James Houston, with the Canadian Guild of Crafts, set up the first co-operative to market these objects in 1959. Now the Inuit themselves run the co-operatives. For most of us, these artefacts of soapstone and other materials are a tangible link with Inuit culture. Somehow, these simple, evocative carvings, made to be picked up and

The dramatic mountains and forests of the Canadian Rockies achieve a new, almost magical beauty with a winter coat of ice and snow.

held, transmit an empathy with the Inuit. The carver, so often removed from the old ways, must have a feeling of strength from the past. In one generation most Inuit have come from a semi-nomadic hunting life into the modern world. Increasingly proud of their uniquely sophisticated culture, and ever adaptable, they have formed the Inuit Tapirisat of Canada – the Inuit Brotherhood – to perpetuate their way of life.

The Northwest Territories

Canada's Inuit live in the immense Northwest Territories. This vast area is, for the most part, above the treeline and about half of it is north of the Arctic Circle. Covering 3 379 684 square kilometres (1 304 974 square miles), it is a lacework of lakes, lowlands, tundra and the polar ice cap, a frozen desert with less than 110 mm (4 inches) of precipitation a year. At first sight the tundra and ice give an appearance of emptiness, but there are many surprises in this land which is, in fact, full of life. Its spectacular beauty is heightened by the long winters of darkness and the short summers of daylight.

On the shore of Great Slave Lake is Yellowknife, capital of the Territories. It was named after the Indians, the Yellowknives (who traded knives of copper) and not after the gold which lies under the city. With its high rises in the "new town" and buildings of c. 1934 in the "old town", it sits prettily on the pink granite rocks of the shore. Local celebrations include a Caribou Carnival and a Midnight Golf Tournament. The latter is held on the weekend closest to June 21, when there is almost continuous daylight. Golfers have to endure playing at midnight on a course that is mostly sand – and the large local ravens who like to make off with the golf balls.

Baffin Island, named after the English explorer William Baffin who explored its coasts in 1615-16, is the largest of the many large islands in the Territories. Most of its inhabitants are Inuit, whose main settlement is at Cape Dorset, while the white population lives at Frobisher Bay. On the island is the only national park above the Arctic Circle – Auyuittuq, the Inuit name for "the place which does not melt". An icefield in the interior highlands occupies one-third of the total area of the park. The park also preserves a large area of spectacular fjords.

In the north-western part of the Territories is the vast delta of the powerful Mackenzie River which flows from Great Slave Lake to the Arctic Ocean. As the river nears the sea it becomes a confused tangle of channels and lakes – half land, half water. The Mackenzie delta is a haven for wildlife – beaver, mink, fox, bear, moose and caribou – and white whales calve in the comparatively warm waters of the delta. However, huge reserves of gas and oil have been found under the Beaufort Sea, so another part of the North will no doubt soon be under assault. Inuvik, on the edge of the delta, with its notable igloo-shaped Roman Catholic church, can be reached from Dawson in the Yukon Territory on the Dempster Highway. This trip necessitates crossing the Mac-

Kluane National Park, in the Yukon, contains some of Canada's highest mountains.

kenzie River by ferry in the summer and by ice bridge in the winter.

Near the border with the Yukon is Nahanni National Park. The park centres on the lower two-thirds – about 386 river kilometres (240 river miles) – of the South Nahanni River and the lower half – 113 river kilometres (70 river miles) – of the Flat River, its main tributary. The Slave Indians, one of the Athabascan tribes, still sometimes exercise their hunting and fishing rights in the area.

Yukon Territory

The Yukon, Canada's vast territory located between the Northwest Territories and Alaska, falls below the treeline, so generally its features differ from those of the Northwest Territories. To most people, the Yukon is the Klondike. Tales of gold-rush days are synonymous with this territory of 536 326 square kilometres (207 088 square miles). Each year 300 000 tourists are drawn to the Yukon by a new interest in the North and by stories of the cruel winter of 1897-98. The Yukon was established in 1898 as a direct result of the gold that was found on the Klon-

dike near Dawson in 1896. Word spread around the world like wildfire and in the winter of 1897-98 more than 29000 men crossed the Chilkoot Pass, high in the Coast Mountains that separate Canada and the United States. Each, by law, had to take in enough supplies for the winter, about 522 kilograms (1150 lb). This meant not one trip over the pass, which at places has a four-in-five gradient, but many trips, perhaps as many as twenty. Few found gold.

Parks Canada is making progress towards the designation of the Chilkoot Trail as a National Historic Park. Enthusiastic tourists climb the Chilkoot Pass, but most go by car or bus on the gravel road via the less steep White Pass. At Carcross there is a cemetery where several of the Yukon's legendary figures are buried – George Carmack, who, with Skookum Jim and Taglish Charley, discovered gold on Rabbit Creek, soon renamed Bonanza. Whitehorse was, of course, founded during the gold rush. It was here that would-be prospectors stopped to dry off after the run through the terrifying Whitehorse rapids. Now the capital is booming and has good restaurants, a museum and a jetport.

At the turn of the century Dawson was known as the "Paris of the North", when a pint of champagne cost 57 grams (2 ounces) of gold. Prospectors have, for the most part, been replaced by tourists. Dawson caters for them with its annual "Discovery Days" and

an establishment called Diamond Tooth Gertie's Gambling Hall, the only legal gambling casino in Canada. Some tourists pan for gold and, when the price of gold increases, the professionals return to stake out the area once again.

Another trail, more important than the one of '98, is the Alaska Highway. It was built in a few short months in 1942 by the US government when it feared a Japanese invasion. The highway crosses the south-west corner of the Yukon and is parallelled by the Alaska Pipeline. Both have brought dramatic changes. Preservationists are keeping a keen eye on these and future developments.

They are also mindful of the needs of Kluane National Park in the south-west. This is one of Canada's most outstanding, with its abundance of wildlife, most notably large mammals, including grizzly and black bears, moose, Dall sheep, mountain goats and caribou. Visitor access is a problem being considered from both viewpoints: the needs of the flora and fauna, and the needs of visitors.

The territory has one of Canada's great rivers, the Yukon, the fifth largest in North America. Riverboats once plied its waters carrying prospectors and settlers. Now visitors enjoy boating and canoeing.

Today some Yukoners work in construction or, perhaps surprisingly, run small farms. Mining, too, is still important. On the heart of every prospector, every miner, indeed every Yukoner, must be engraved at least a few lines of the poetry of the Canadian Scot Robert Service. Critics sniffed at his poetry when it was published. But millions, who had never been to the Yukon, and would never go there, knew that he had distilled the essence.

> "This is the law of the Yukon, that only the strong shall thrive;
> That surely the Weak shall perish, and only the Fit survive.
> Dissolute, damned and despairful, crippled and palsied and slain,
> This is the will of the Yukon, —Lo, how she makes it plain."

The Indians of the Yukon are of the Athabascan language group, and make up one-quarter of the total Yukon population of 23000. Twelve native communities have survived and undoubtedly will continue to survive, because these people have a determination to be part of the future. The Council for Yukon Indians is at present negotiating a land-claims deal worth millions of dollars with the Federal Government. Here, at least, there will almost certainly be an acceptable solution to the problem of reconciling two widely different lifestyles, that of Indian and non-Indian. Perhaps finally the Indians will refute the distorted image of the cowboy movies, and at the same time cast aside the deprivation that is so common among the native peoples of today.

And the oil flows on – bringing energy, wealth and disruption. Hundreds of years ago, this future was unknowingly foretold when the Inuit told whalers strange stories of black lakes that burned.

possessions, and hunting became very much easier. The image was created of the Indian on a fiery steed. The almost total obliteration of the magnificent buffalo by the white man, accelerated by the coming of the railway, sealed the fate of the Plains people.

Horses are still much in evidence particularly around Calgary, in the foothills of the Rockies, where Alberta's Calgary Stampede is held every year. It is one of the greatest shows on earth, where cowboys test their skills against each other by riding bucking broncos, by roping cows and by competing in the Chuckwagon Races. The Calgarians have a flair for showmanship which more than matches their sound business sense.

Edmonton, Alberta's capital, is located in the valley of the South Sasketchewan River. It is another great centre for the oil industry, including the Athabascan Tar Sands which lay to the north. Edmonton's annual "Klondike Days" celebrate the gold rush, a boom time for the city, when it earned its title "gateway to the north". The Provincial Museum in the city has a particularly good display on the Prairie Indians. In the Badlands of southern Alberta is Dinosaur Provincial Park. No area in the world is as rich in dinosaur remains, as is this moonscape setting. Visitors can travel the Dinosaur Trail and see partially excavated dinosaur fossils.

A touching sidelight on Canadian history is recalled at Lethbridge, in southern Alberta. During the Second World War thousands of Japanese-Canadians were interned near here, and their property and homes in BC sold off. After the war many chose to stay, and the charming Nikka Yuko Centennial Garden has been built, a symbol of Japanese-Canadian friendship.

Cypress Hills, straddling the Alberta-Sasketchewan border has had a turbulent history. It was a last refuge for the buffalo and for the Indians. Even today it is similar to an island, environmentally, because it has flora and fauna native to places hundreds of kilometres away. Here white men peddled illegal alcohol to the Indians. It was after the slaughter of a group of Indians by white hunters, that Sir John A. Macdonald, Canada's first Prime Minister, established the North-West Mounted Police, later renamed the Royal Canadian Mounted Police. The Indians were impressed with the way the new police force handled the situation, and the fine reputation of the Mounties was established.

Another episode of the Old West was enacted here when Sitting Bull brought his warriors to Cypress Hills after the Battle of the Little Big Horn (1876). To enforce Canadian law, Inspector James Walsh with four constables and two scouts rode into Sitting Bull's camp of about 4000 warriors. Walsh's courage won the respect of the Indians, although it was to be another four years before Sitting Bull could be persuaded to return to the United States. His fears were confirmed for he was killed shortly after his return.

The Royal Canadian Mounted Police Barracks in Regina, capital of Sasketchewan, is where recruits spend the first six months of their training. It was on this site that the French-Canadian Louis Riel was executed for murder in 1885, after leading the North-West Rebellion and attempting to set up a provisional

Farmers in Saskatchewan employ big machines to dominate big spaces.

government to safeguard the rights of the Métis (people of mixed European and Indian origin). Regina was first called Pile O' Bones, because the site was where, for countless years, the Indians and Métis had driven the buffalo to their deaths. The CPR line passed here, so the capital was moved from Battleford to Pile O' Bones. When the first train went through, with Princess Louise on board, she re-named it Regina after her mother Queen Victoria.

The prosperous farmers of today are descendants of those who survived the first winters, often near starvation. They had been drawn to the West by the offer of free land – a quarter section of nearly 65 hectares (160 acres) to every male over eighteen – and the promise of religious freedom. There are people alive who remember turning the first tough sod. They or their children had to withstand the almost equally difficult period of the Depression years. The economic disaster was compounded by a terrible drought. The dust-storms started in 1929 and it seemed that they would never end. On land so flat that people imagine they can see the curvature of the Earth, it became impossible to see from house to barn even at midday.

The ribbon of the Trans-Canada highway passing hundreds of kilometres of golden grain, reveals little of this earlier period. However, in Saskatoon, there is a good example of the single-mindedness of these people. Wishing to be able to ski near their city, they have built their own ski hill on the rolling Prairies – Mount Blackstrap, which is 91 metres (299 feet) high and dominates the surrounding landscape.

Manitoba with its large lakes – Lakes Winnipeg, Manitoba and Winnipegosis – is a Prairie province with a considerable amount of water. The capital, Winnipeg, was originally a French fur-traders' post, situated at the confluence of the Red and Assiniboine Rivers. Winnipeg was for many years the financial and distribution centre for western Canada. It still has Canada's most important grain exchange and is the headquarters of the Hudson's Bay Company. An important cultural centre, this city is most famous for the Royal Winnipeg Ballet. In the Manitoba Museum of Man and Nature there is a Subarctic gallery, with displays on the polar bears which build their snow dens on the shores of Hudson Bay, and exhibits on the north Manitoban town of Churchill.

Central Canada

Ontario: Land of Lakes

Over the border and into the Lake of the Woods area is Ontario. During the Depression years hobos travelling the rails had a name for Canada – Big Lonely. In northern Ontario with its thousands of lakes, hundreds of thousands of hectares of pine forests, the name seems appropriate. The eerie cry of the loon against a solid backdrop of pine trees, the honking of geese, the howling of wolves, the dip of the paddle in the cool, dark water make one's spine tingle. These wild places are a haven for birds and animals, and such wildernesses as Quetico Provincial Park preserve it all. Quetico, north-west of Lake Superior, has hundreds of kilometres of canoe routes. Indian place-names abound for this was the land of the Ojibwa.

In the 1920s the northern wilderness of this province was depicted in a new and exciting way by the Group of Seven, artists who abandoned the gentle European landscape style to paint trees, rocks and water in a new, raw and dynamic way. A collection of their paintings can be seen at the McMichael Canadian Collection in Kleinburg, just north of Toronto.

There are immense mineral deposits in the Canadian Shield which geologically forms much of Ontario. This, combined with forestry, gives Ontario's north a strong basis of wealth for the present and for the future. Ontario is the commercial, financial and governmental centre of Canada, a cause for resentment in some areas of this vast country. Central to all this activity are the Great Lakes, the world's largest surface of fresh water, and one of the great natural features of the North American continent. This water is vital to the cities of Ontario, including Hamilton for steel, Windsor for cars and Thunder Bay for grain. And then there in Toronto.

Toronto, on the shore of Lake Ontario, is Canada's leading city in terms of commerce and finance. Diverse industrially, rich culturally, it is also a wonderfully free city. Exuberance is surfacing in the souls of Torontonians whether they are attending the Carabana, the annual West Indian festival on Centre Island, skating on the frozen Nathan Phillips Square rink, dining in Ed's Warehouse, madly cheering at a hockey game in Maple Leaf Gardens, exploring the new and imaginative zoo, or taking in the summer Caravan festival which celebrates the more than seventy ethnic groups that co-exist here. During the latter, one can dine and be entertained by a different group at almost any time day or night – as long as your energy lasts. This human element is in contrast to the sophisticated boutiques, sleek, towering bank buildings and super-highways. It is a city where each New Year's Eve everyone is invited to ride for free on the transit system.

In addition to the tens of thousands of lakes in the north of the province, there are many close to the big cities, which almost empty each Friday night during the summer. There are traffic jams on every road north as people head for their summer cottages, usually in the lakeland regions of Muskoka, Haliburton, or Kawartha. And there is Algonquin Provincial Park, so popular that you have to make a reservation to canoe through any of its 1 600 kilometres (994 miles) of canoe routes. Canoeists are issued with garbage bags on the way in; they must return them full on the way out – one way of preventing a popular area from becoming spoiled.

Near Belleville is Prince Edward County, a fascinating peninsula which pushes out into Lake Ontario for a distance of 40 kilometres (25 miles). It contains farms, orchards and, surprisingly, two sand dune systems, the latter forming part of Sandbanks

Provincial Park. Dunes reach 20 metres (66 feet) in height, and provide a habitat for plants and animals not normally found in this part of Canada.

As with so many other places in Canada, nostalgic Kingston at the north-east end of Lake Ontario was founded as a French fur-trading post in 1673. It was deserted by the French after the Battle of the Plains of Abraham, but was later settled by United Empire Loyalists at the time of the American War of Independence. It is to this period that it owes its charm, and to the fact that it was, for a few brief years, the capital of Canada. Its limestone houses and Parliament Building built in 1843-44, now the City Hall, remain and add to the feeling of a place that has been touched by greatness, then left to pursue another destiny. Its destiny lay another way – as a quiet university town, also famous for its federal penitentiary and the Cathedral of St George, supposedly a miniature version of St Paul's in London. Kingston has fortifications which date from the War of 1812; when the Americans arrived they were somewhat surprised to find that the staunch Loyalists had no intention of being "liberated". To this day the city has a military presence. Battle-ready ships that perished in a sudden squall during the War of 1812, when the Americans were driven back to their own land, have been discovered on the bottom of western Lake Ontario. The *Hamilton* and the *Scourge* were merchant ships which the United States converted to warships, and hence were top-heavy with guns. They are intact, sitting almost upright on the sandy bottom, waiting for the day they will be recovered.

As Lake Ontario begins to narrow at its eastern end, hundreds of rocks and islands emerge picturesquely from the water. The Thousand Islands, and there are about 1000 of them depending on how you define an island, are scattered over a distance of 50 kilometres (31 miles). Around and between them flows the traffic of the St Lawrence Seaway, borne along on one of the world's great waterways. The International Boundary Line also flows between the islands, and the Seaway project was a joint Canadian-United States development. As such it was opened by Queen Elizabeth II and President Eisenhower in 1959. Thus 3768 kilometres (2341 miles) of waterways for ocean-going vessels was opened up and 15286 kilometres (9499 miles) of water for leisure activities.

At Morrisburg on the St Lawrence River is Upper Canada Village, probably the finest of the many such pioneer villages in Canada. The homes and other buildings, some moved here before the flooding that was necessary during the construction of the Seaway project, are bustling with activities commonplace in this part of Canada from 1784 to 1867, the year of Canada's Confederation.

Canada's capital, Ottawa, is beautifully placed with its Parliament Buildings overlooking both the Rideau Canal and the Ottawa River. A pleasant city, it is noted for its riverside drives, tulips in the spring, Changing the Guard on Parliament Hill in the summer, trips to see the brilliantly coloured leaves in the fall, and skating on the Rideau Canal in the winter. Ottawa, in addition to its governmental role, has become an exciting cultural centre.

La Belle Province

Hull, with its bright lights, is just across the Ottawa, or Outaouais, River in Quebec, *la belle province*. This river has been the highway linking this area with Montreal since the days of the explorers and the voyageurs. Samuel de Champlain came this way in the early seventeenth century, as did Dollard des Ormeaux and Pierre-Esprit Radisson. The forests around the Ottawa and Gatineau rivers, with their sawmills and lumberjacks, are part of the folklore of Canada.

To the north lies untamed wilderness, to the east Montreal and to the north the Laurentian Mountains, which form the south-eastern edge of the Canadian Shield. Directly north-west of Montreal itself, these mountains provide a rich winter sports area for the thriving metropolis. The *P'tit Train des Neiges* (Little Snow Train) takes skiers from Montreal to within a few metres of the cross-country trails, which stretch for 2000 kilometres (1243 miles). In addition, there are thirty downhill ski centres with Mont Tremblant, the highest mountain in the Laurentians, as the focal point. Summer and winter there are festivals and theatre, as well as special sports events.

The city of Montreal is indisputably one of the great cities of North America. Situated on and around two islands, Montréal and Jésus, it is surrounded by the waters of the St Lawrence and its tributaries. The Indians fully appreciated the fine site at the confluence of three rivers, for here they had built a settlement, Hochelaga. When the first Europeans arrived, these people were firmly ensconced, and thriving, in their circular stockade. Modern Montreal excitingly combines history and modern technology, and not just one culture, or two, but many. Built around Mount Royal (Mont Réal), it seems somewhat like a series of villages, which often have an ethnic basis. Montreal is a centre of business, the dramatic arts, religion, culinary excellence – and politics. The so-called "Quiet Revolution" of the 1960s probably had a greater impact in Quebec than in many other places in North America. For here traditions were stronger, the impact of Church and family greater.

There is now a subterranean Montreal, a clever way to defeat the extremely cold winters. Passageways link the main stores and hotels, as well as providing 1000 boutiques, 100 bars and restaurants, and a number of theatres and cinemas.

The Eastern Townships, east of Montreal, are, like many areas along the south shore, a place where Loyalists chose to settle after the American War of Independence. In this green agricultural country there are the Loyalists' solid stone houses, the Québeçois shrines to the Virgin Mary beside the roadside, sugaring-off parties in the maple sugar bushes each spring, and craft centres which feature the woodcarvings for which Quebec is famous. There are churches and parks, great rivers and waterfalls,

Balsam Lake, near Kirkfield, forms part of Ontario's 177000 square kilometres (nearly 70000 square miles) of lakes.

summer theatres and antique shops.

On the north shore, Montreal is linked to Quebec City, the much older settlement, by a road which dates from 1737 – the Chemin du Roi or King's Road. Quebec City, dramatically placed on the sharply ascending heights above the St Lawrence, is North America's most historic city and certainly one of the most beautiful. In 1535-36 the French navigator Jacques Cartier wintered here and, in 1608, Champlain built the first permanent European residence. This area, at the foot of the cliff, is preserved as Place Royale. A church now stands on the site of Champlain's residence, surrounded by historic buildings, a museum and an art gallery.

Because of its strategic position the city had the large population of 2000 in the early eighteenth century. After the Battle of the Plains of Abraham in 1759, the French-speaking people of Canada were set on a new course. Immigration from Britain followed, as well as an influx of Loyalists. In 1861 forty per cent of the population was English-speaking. Today that figure has shrunk to four per cent. In Vieux Québec, the old city, there is a fantastic atmosphere created by beauty and history and entertainment.

Farms and communities nestle all along the

St Lawrence, the nurturing, all-encompassing source of life. There is a boat trip up the Saguenay River with its sheer cliffs and a statue of the Virgin Mary, now an historic monument, dramatically placed. The river leads to Lac Saint-Jean, where Indians from many nations once met to barter. The many Indian place names in this area reflect this history. Ashuapmouchouan means "place where one lies in wait for the moose", and Péribonka "he who paves his road through the sand". The Indians may have been attracted by the wild blueberries for which the region is famous. Thousands of hectares are now cultivated and at Mistassinni, north of Lac Saint-Jean, there is a Blueberry Festival every August. The highlight is a 136-kilogram (300-lb) pie which is paraded through the streets.

In the last few years, Canada has become a land of festivals. Often the festivals are linked with history, or the celebrations focus on a local feature, famous person or agricultural crop. And then there are the festivals that have been conceived with an outrageous sense of humour and a simple wish to have a party. One such is the Mosquito Festival, held at Notre-Dame-des-Monts each June.

Quebec's far north is a vast area with immense natural resources. A most powerful symbol of modern Quebec is the colossal hydro-electric project – La Grande Complex, east of James Bay. Here, in the most monumental project of its kind ever undertaken in North America, giant dams have been built and spillways blasted out of solid rock, as was the world's largest underground powerhouse, which was inaugurated in 1979. The Cree Indians, who for thousands of years have lived as nomads in this area, have been compensated in money, land, and hunting and fishing rights over a vast area, some of which is located near the new reservoirs. And they, too, are employed on the construction work.

The Gaspé Peninsula, a northern extension of the Appalachian range, is surrounded by the waters of the Gulf of St Lawrence. It has seen much history pass by – Vikings, Basque fishermen, Cartier, Champlain and others. The peninsula was first known as *Gachepe* derived from *Gespeg*, meaning "the ends of the earth". Later came the English settlers, then Scots, men from Jersey and Guernsey, and some shipwrecked Irish. For centuries boats were the only means of communication. The railway came in 1876, leading to forestry, emigration, immigration and tourism. With its sandy beaches and rivers full of salmon, the peninsula was considered for a time to be the "Canadian riviera", with yachts and summer mansions. Today the people are keen on promoting tourism, and a road encircles the peninsula along the dramatic coast, making Parc de la Gaspésie and Parc National de Forillon accessible.

Out in the Gulf, north-west of Cape Breton Island, Nova Scotia, is one of Canada's surprises – the Iles de la Madeleine, or Magdalen Islands, which are part of *la province de Québec*. This little known string of islands has 300 kilometres (186 miles) of sandy beaches. Here too history has swept over the land, ultimately leaving it in peace and the people to survive on fish and shipwrecks. The tradition of colourfully painted houses, scattered haphazardly over the terrain, goes back to the days when only boat paint was readily available. Boat and house got a coat of paint at the same time. Fishing for lobsters is now a lucrative industry.

The Atlantic Provinces

Canada's four eastern provinces are dominated by the great Atlantic Ocean. Whether the landscape be rugged and dramatic as in Newfoundland, or peaceful and agricultural like Prince Edward Island, most people live in close proximity to the sea. In fact it is difficult to be far from it. Over the centuries fishing has been a mainstay, and it is much the same today.

The beautiful natural environment of New Brunswick attracts tourists, hunters and fishermen. The interior of the province is thickly populated with trees, so forestry is a major industry. There is a large French-speaking minority, descendants of Acadians who returned after their ancestors had been harshly driven from this land by British forces. Settlers came from Germany, and the Pennsylvania-Dutch from the United States with other Loyalists settlers. In fact the Loyalists arrived in great numbers. For example, in 1783, 3000 arrived in a fleet of square-rigged ships, some of a total of 14000.

Charming Fredericton, capital of New Brunswick, which contains early Victorian gingerbread houses, has a slow, comfortable way of life and is sometimes called the "Poets' Corner" of Canada. Art galleries like the Beaverbrook Gallery also encourage the arts. New Brunswick is famous for its tidal bore which can be seen in several places, two being Moncton and Saint John. The Bay of Fundy tidal bore is the strongest in the world. Saint John is also a manufacturing centre, a port, and a railway terminus. It has a drydock viewing platform, befitting the place that used to be known as the "Liverpool of America". The life of the Acadian people is depicted at the Village Historique Acadien, near Caraquet, in the north-east. A festival is opened by the Blessing of the Fleet. Boats come from all over the province to be blessed by the Bishop of Halifax, a poignant reminder of the almost mystical regard for the sea.

Nova Scotia, or "New Scotland", has the added ingredient of a solid and determined core of Scottish ancestry. Here one can find the language of Scotland, Scottish music and Scottish dances, culminating in an annual Gathering of the Clans, a magnificent occasion that makes hearts almost burst with pride. Halifax, the capital, is one of Canada's great harbours, a feature which first attracted the British. This port is always open, even when ice blocks the St Lawrence, and it has always had a military importance. Here Edward, Duke of Kent, was Commander-in-Chief for six years, before he married and became the father of the girl who was to become Queen Victoria.

In a few places schooners are still hand-crafted, in the tradition of the famous trophy-winning *Bluenose*, built in 1921. The *Bluenose* may have been the fastest fishing schooner ever to have sailed the Atlantic and its unbeaten record is celebrated by a picture on the Canadian dime. Boats are being built in back yards and harbours all over the province. Although most are of fibreglass and plywood, the boatbuilders have as much pride in their work and love of the sea as any others.

Beautiful Cape Breton Island has some of Canada's most outstanding parks, Cape Breton Highlands National Park, encircled by the Cabot Trail, and the National Historic Park at Louisbourg. In pride of place in the latter is the Fortress of Louisbourg in the south-east. So threatening a feature was this imposing structure to the English-speaking settlers that it was forced to surrender in 1749. It was eventually, unbelievably, given back to the French, only to be recaptured again in 1758. This time it was almost totally destroyed, serving as a quarry for stone. But those inhabitants of so long ago could never have imagined that it would be rebuilt some 200 years later, thus enabling visitors to get a vivid picture of life in the mid-eighteenth century. This reconstruction project is certainly one of the largest undertaken anywhere. To the people there is something so special about this difficult, intriguing province, that if, by some quirk of fate, they are compelled to live elsewhere, they yearn for the rocks and the sea.

In complete contrast, tiny Prince Edward Island, sitting 14.5 kilometres (9 miles) out in the Gulf, manages to exude a gentle tranquillity. It is a place of good harvests – that sensible staple, potatoes, and feasts of lobster and oyster. There are scenic drives with such names as Lady Slipper and Blue Heron, and it is here, in Canada's smallest province, that Lucy Maud Montgomery set her famous story, *Anne of Green Gables*.

PEI can also lay claim to having hosted the first meeting of the Fathers of Confederation. This meeting took place in 1864, the intention being to discuss Maritime union, although representatives from Ontario and Quebec came too. Canada's Confederation followed in 1867. The stubborn islanders of the "Cradle of Confederation" held out until 1873, when they too became part of the Dominion. In the provincial capital of Charlottetown a Confederation Centre commemorates these events, as does the actual meeting room in Province House.

The Micmac Indians, who once lived here and elsewhere in the Maritimes, have survived, unlike the Beothucks of Newfoundland who were wiped out. The Micmacs live on a small island in Malpeque Bay.

Distinctively set off from the rest of North America by the 18-kilometre (11-mile) wide Strait of Belle Isle, the island of Newfoundland is, in every sense, more of the sea than of the land. The names of the villages in the bays, coves and inlets aptly express the individuality of the people and the hardness of life – Useless Bay, Cuckold Cove, Little Heart's Ease

Rivers and streams cut through New Brunswick's Fundy National Park, which extends for 13 kilometres (8 miles) along the Bay of Fundy.

and Bay Despair, originally Baie d'Espoir (Bay of Hope). The island has 9660 kilometres (6003 miles) of deeply indented and rugged coastline, where little harbours provide sanctuary for the fishing vessels which were the mainstay of life here before the twentieth century. And things have not changed that much.

It was the Grand Banks, the most extensive fishing grounds in the world, which drew fishermen from Europe long before the explorers came. And long before the fishermen, there were the Vikings. Along the eastern seaboard of North America and sometimes quite far inland, there are hopeful claims of Viking sites. But the only Viking settlement in the New World, which has been proven and excavated, is at L'Anse aux Meadows on the most northerly tip of the island. This priceless site is now a National Historic Park.

At least 7000 wrecks lie off these rugged shores. The rusted hulks of some, like the *Ethie*, can still be seen. The story is the stuff of legends. This steamer foundered in a storm in 1919, and as she began to break up, the captain drove her towards shore and grounded her. A lifeline attached to a breeches buoy

was thrown over the side. A dog swam out from shore, carried the line back and all 120 people were saved. Such events, and more tragic ones, are celebrated in song and story for generations to come.

It is to the sea that people turn for sustenance. Mining and forestry are important, but somehow not quite enough. Mines may close or forests disappear, but the sea will never let them down. For the fish of the Grand Banks have shaped the province and the people. The population is of about ninety-five per cent British origin. For so long insular, speech patterns may, fascinatingly, recall rural Elizabethan England.

At St John's, fishing boats have moored for half a millennium. In the early years it was governed by a Fishing Admiral – the captain of the first ship to arrive in the fishing season. St John's is an extraordinarily different provincial capital, where some of the houses cling haphazardly to the rocky headlands of the harbour, always looking out to sea.

The island of Newfoundland joined with Labrador on the mainland to become Canada's tenth province in 1949. Labrador, adjoining Quebec, is a treeless domain, frozen for much of the year. Strangely, it almost mimics the shape of the island. Labrador is largely uninhabited, although there are a few settlements along the coast and near the iron ore mines. The vastness of the rest is left for the animals of Canada's North. Untarnished, unspoiled, it is a precious resource for Canada and for the world.

The North

"There is a brilliance to the sun above the 60th parallel that is a startling change from the soft, summer haze of more southerly latitudes. Maybe it is the mountain weather, or perhaps the constantly shifting patterns of light and dark, but a Yukon summer sky reminds you of a child's painting, with clouds standing sharply out against the blue."

John and Janet Foster, nature writers, photographers

"In the spring when the sun never sets
And when calm glassy waters roamed the morning seas,
Oh, those were the happy times.

When the birds and seals
Lived only for playing,
Oh, those were the happy times.

When we would stay up all night,
Looking for birds' nests,
Oh, those were the happy times.

When the sun began to warm the morning air
And my sister could no longer keep her eyes open,
Oh, those were the happy times.

When I, too, fought the coming of sleep,
But my dreams would win in the end,
Oh, those were the happy times."

Lucy Evaloardjuak, Eskimo resident of Pond Inlet

Some of Canada's Inuit are returning to the challenge and the joy of the Hunt.

Opposite, top: The Mackenzie Mountains in Nahanni National Park are one of the three mountain ranges through which the South Nahanni River flows.

Opposite, bottom: A group explores South Nahanni River in rubber "canoes". To the Slave tribe of Athabascan Indians the river was always Nahadeh – Powerful River, a river whose magic force was able to connect the spirit of man with that of nature. Within the park's 4765 square kilometres (1840 square miles) there is much that is memorable and powerful: canyon systems among the deepest on Earth, hoodoos (mushroom-shaped rocks), hot springs, seemingly bottomless lakes, and extensive cave systems. In 1979 UNESCO proclaimed Nahanni National Park the first World Heritage Site, to be preserved for all mankind.

Below: Caribou gather at Repulse Bay, Northwest Territories. Herds as large as 100000 annually migrate 1900 kilometres (1180 miles) within the Canadian and American North. This prehistoric trek takes them from winter to summer feeding grounds and back, and has convinced the Canadian and United States governments to work out a joint caribou management policy. Caribou are admirably suited for the North because of their coarse, compact hair. Their fur is the warmest known.

Above: *Within Kluane National Park, the scale is so immense that whole forests are dwarfed.*

Opposite, top: *Kathleen Lake is in Kluane National Park, in the Yukon. Kluane has some of the world's largest glaciers outside the polar region, and its mountains are home to the best collection of wild large mammals in North America. The park of 22000 square kilometres (8500 square miles) was established in 1972 in the south-west corner of the Territory. As with most of Canada's North, it is ecologically sensitive to intrusions.*

Opposite, bottom: *Virginia Falls is in Nahanni National Park, Northwest Territories. Untouched, unharnessed, Virginia Falls is one of the continent's superlatives. The South Nahanni River explodes over the falls, which are more than one and a half times the height of Niagara. The portion of the river on the south side plunges 90 metres (295 feet) straight down, while the centre smashes against a pillar of limestone, and the north falls 52 metres (171 feet). Often rainbow crosses rainbow in the resulting fury of water and mist.*

The West Coast

". . . the British Columbian, no matter how heartily gregarious he may seem, sees himelf dramatically as a loner in a world of loners."

George Woodcock, writer, critic and social historian

"The truth [about Victoria] will be found in no document, photograph, painting, poem, or song, but you may stumble upon it, some spring evening, in a little garden where an old man is pruning a hedge; in a quiet house a-glisten with family plate and dark English oak; in a secondhand store on Fort Street, cluttered with the heirlooms of dead Victorians; in a field of white lilies, blue camassia, and yellow buttercups under the crooked limbs of a native oak; in the park where the children are feeding crusts to the swans and the air is sweet with the perfume of plum blossom, broom, sea salt, and ageless conifers; or again on a winter night when the white rollers are pounding in from the Pacific and the big foghorns are moaning."

Bruce Hutchison, author and journalist.

"Next time I paint Indians I'm going off on a tangent tear. There is something bigger than fact: the underlying spirit, all it stands for, the mood, the vastness, the wilderness, the Western breath of a go-to-the-devil-if-you-don't-like-it, the eternal big spaceness of it. Oh the West! I'm of it and I love it."

Emily Carr, painter

Kokanee Creek, near Nelson, is framed by British Columbia's forests and mountains.

Above: *A number of strong images are associated with British Columbia. Among the most powerful are totem poles, and wildlife, such as the increasingly rare bald eagle. Totem poles, remarkably similar to coats-of-arms, were erected by the West Coast Indians in front of their massive cedar homes or, as here, in burial grounds. Animals and birds, like the eagle, were represented on the totem poles. Here the symbolic and the real merge.*

Left: *One of the most beautiful spots on the Alaska Highway is Muncho Lake, where the aquamarine water reflects the surrounding mountains. The Highway was built in 1942 by the United States government to link Alaska and the Yukon with roads farther south. Fear of a Japanese invasion spurred on construction. In eight months 2451 kilometres (1523 miles) of highway were built.*

Diana Creek, near Prince Rupert on the north coast of British Columbia, shows forestry's pattern of destruction and renewal.

British Columbia's harbours are a haven for work and pleasure craft. Recreational boating is extremely popular. At the end of 1982, 1.8 million small boats (10 horse-power or more) were registered with the Department of Transport. Vast numbers of smaller craft abound. Small harbours on Canada's east and west coasts require constant maintenance against the ceaseless action of the sea and shifting sandbars. In some places in British Columbia floating breakwaters have been installed to protect exposed wharves.

A rain forest grows in Pacific Rim National Park, Vancouver Island. In this forest, unique in Canada, massive redwoods reach toward the sun, and on these great trees lives a variety of highly specialized plant life. All thrive due to the warm Japan current, moderate temperatures and heavy rainfall.

Above: *Bursting spring blossoms frame the inner harbour in front of the Empress Hotel, Victoria, Vancouver Island. The Empress is a symbol of the Britishness of British Columbia. Springtime comes to Victoria much earlier than in the rest of Canada. When daffodils bloom here, most points east are still in the icy grip of winter.*

Left: *Butchart Gardens, north of Victoria, are named after Mrs Jenny Butchart who created beauty from the large and ugly hole that had been her husband's lime quarry. Now much expanded and world famous there is a Sunken Garden, a Rose Garden and a Japanese Garden.*

Above: *Slocan Lake, near Nelson, is located between two of British Columbia's mountain ranges – the Monashee Mountains on the west and the Selkirk Mountains on the east.*

Opposite, top: *This section of the Fraser River Canyon is near Lillooet, British Columbia. "We had to pass where no man should venture," said Simon Fraser of the wild and turbulent river named after him. When gold was discovered in the area in 1858 the government of the newly created province of British Columbia decided to build a road, because the river was so impossible. The result was the Cariboo Wagon Road from which this view can be seen.*

Opposite, bottom: *Lake O'Hara is in the Yoho National Park. Deck chairs are gently blanketed with snow as a summer scene is transformed into one of winter beauty.*

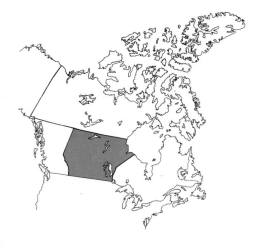

The Prairie Provinces

"When I was growing up in the prairies in the mid-Twenties and early Thirties, we were taught in school that the sunsets of Manitoba were the most spectacular in the world, and we believed it. Climate was extreme, either hot or cold, and everything around us unfolded without ambiguity or shading. If you grow up among oceanic fields of wheat, tossed between extremes of summer and winter, you never learn to value the happy medium, and no matter where you live afterward you never stop yearning for the old totality of space."

Miriam Waddington, poet

"And the next day they still ran along the prairie, but now the land broke into rolling country ('This *must* be the Rolling Prairie!'), and the world became lightly wooded again. Then, beyond increasingly high hills they looked westward and saw, coldly blue and white against the sky, a tumult of mountains.

"In the gullies of the little hills through which they now passed there were aspens and birches whose leaves the early frost had turned from green to gold. The birches with their white maidenly stems and honey-yellow leaves shone against the dark conifers. Far to the north of them, but still east of the Rockies, east of Jasper House, the Athabasca River flowed widely through a land that was all gold. Golden golden golden shone the birch trees in the sunshine in that northern land from north to south, from east to west, spiked here and there by dark conifers. Few travellers along the brave steel way had ever heard of this golden world."

Ethel Wilson, novelist and short story writer

At Olds near Calgary, Alberta, the sun-washed stubble is set against the cloud-darkened sky.

Above: *Angel Glacier flows down Mount Edith Cavell in Jasper National Park, western Alberta. The glacier was so named because its shape, as it pours out of a rock basin, resembles spread wings. Jasper National Park contains some breathtaking Rocky Mountain scenery. Mount Edith Cavell is in sight of the town of Jasper, which is located where the Athabasca River meets the Miette.*

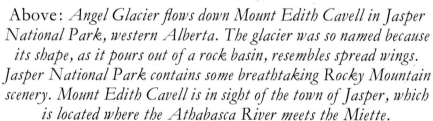

Right: *This view of Columbia Icefield, Jasper National Park, shows a point where solid becomes liquid. The Icefield Parkway, which links Banff and Jasper, comes close to the ice, and tourists can take a snowmobile tour of a glacier. The icefield, which tops the Continental Divide, covers 310 square kilometres (120 square miles). There are nine major glaciers in this area, the waters of which flow into three oceans.*

Above: *Waterfall Lake and Mount Chephren are in Banff National Park. The thrusting mountains form a perfect backdrop for the numerous small, exquisite lakes. The snow lies in horizontal ridges on the mountains in this area, giving a striped effect.*

Opposite, top: *Big Horn River cuts through the Rockies, and its deep canyon collects run-off water from the surrounding area.*

Opposite, bottom: *Canada's rail links are essential for transporting such products as pulp and paper to markets. In fact, it was the promise of the building of the Canadian Pacific Railway that brought British Columbia into Confederation in 1871. The actual construction of the railway from 1881 to 1885 broke all records for the speed of track-laying by manual labour in the Prairies, while north of Lake Superior in Ontario, and in the Rockies of British Columbia and Alberta, seemingly insurmountable difficulties were at times encountered. The lines over Kicking Horse Pass, Rogers' Pass and the Fraser Canyon are still considered to be remarkable achievements.*

Above: *At the Stoney Wilderness Centre, about 214 kilometres (133 miles) south of Jasper, an Indian woman prepares a buffalo hide. Calgary's famous Glenbow Museum has displays of Indian and Inuit artefacts.*

Opposite, top: *The green waters of Lake Hector, in the Stoney Wilderness Centre, spread below land that is beautifully forested.*

Opposite, bottom: *The Calgary Tower oversees the downtown core of the city with its 191 metres (626 feet) of height. Every hour the restaurant on top completes another revolution. Oil was first discovered in Canada's West near Calgary in 1947. Now the city is the headquarters for several hundred oil-related companies.*

Opposite, top: *These wheat elevators are at Ponoka, south of Edmonton. Each grain pool company paints its elevators a distinctive, and distinctly cheerful, colour. Ponoka has its own museum, Fort Ostell, which was built to protect settlers during the Riel Rebellion.*

Opposite, bottom: *Alberta is known as the "rodeo province", the most famous rodeo being the Calgary Exhibition and Stampede. The extensive grounds are one of the landmarks to be seen from the Calgary Tower (page 48). Here the world's best ride bucking broncos, rope cows and compete in the thrilling Chuckwagon Races. Cowboys test their skills at rodeos in other towns of the West, but the Calgary Stampede is the one that matters.*

Below: *Round-ups and cattle drives symbolize the old West. Cattle remain important in the economy, following wheat and oil. Calgary, sometimes called Cowtown, has long been a transportation and meat-packing centre. These stockyards and the Burns plant are one facet of a dynamic city.*

Fort Edmonton, once a major fur-trading post, has been reconstructed within Fort Edmonton Park. In the park there are historical villages representing the city at various stages in its development (left). There is also an Indian village (above) where the tepees and the camp-fire smoke are placed against the park's fine setting beside the North Saskatchewan River.

Each July the city of Edmonton celebrates its history during the gold-rush with "Klondike Days" when, among other things, a "King of the Klondike" is chosen. Other annual festivities include a folk-music festival and a children's festival.

*Beneath Medicine Hat, Alberta, is a reservoir of natural gas which
has been exploited since the 1880s. When Rudyard Kipling visited
here in 1907, he described it as a place "with all hell for a
basement", a thought which may have encouraged the building of such
impressive churches. The gas which was accidentally discovered by a
CPR crew drilling for water now provides low-cost utilities, a great
boost for the city. Gas is only one of the many natural resources
hidden beneath the prairie soils. Oil, uranium, zinc, cadmium and
copper are among the others.*

*The hoodoos in Writing-on-Stone Provincial Park are strange
sandstone formations which are continually being sculpted by wind
and water. The mushroom-shaped hoodoos are a symbol of
Alberta's badlands. In the park a number of native carvings on
stone – petroglyphs – and rock paintings – pictographs – decorate
the sandstone cliffs along the Milk River. Naturalists conduct
tours through the valley which is a natural sanctuary for wild life.
In the distance can be seen the Sweetgrass Hills of Montana.*

Prince Albert National Park is 56 kilometres (35 miles) from Prince Albert and close to the geographical centre of Saskatchewan. Here the aspen forest mixes with the boreal wilderness and there are pockets of virgin prairie grassland. On the latter live coyotes, badgers and ground squirrels. There is a small herd of buffalo, and visitors can sightsee from a paddle-steamer on Lake Waskesiu.

Opposite: *A pioneer church at North Battleford, Saskatchewan, an interesting historical village of the 1925 era, which is a branch of the Western Development Museum. Across the valley of the North Saskatchewan River is Battleford, once the capital. The latter's National Historic Park has as its focal point a restored North-West Mounted Police station.*

Above: *Lake Winnipeg is a vast inland waterway. In a little
known chapter of Canadian history, steamboats – called "fire
canoes" by the astonished Indians – used to ply these waters. Each
summer tourists gather at Selkirk to cruise on* Lord Selkirk II.

Opposite, top: *Manitoba's Riding Mountain National Park is a
place where three environments meet – northern, western and
eastern. It was here on the "mountain", part of the Manitoba
escarpment, that fur-traders exchanged canoes for horses.*

Opposite, bottom: *Whirlpool Lake, one of Manitoba's 100 000
lakes, is on the eastern side of Riding Mountain National Park.
This wealth of water encourages such activities as canoeing on a
misty morning. It is also responsible for a great diversity of wildlife.
Elk, moose and bears abound.*

Overleaf: *The Legislative Building on the Assiniboine River,
Winnipeg, was built in 1919 of Manitoba Tyndall limestone. The
style is neo-classical revival, then popular for important buildings.
The main stairway within is flanked by two bronze buffalo, in
tribute to those far-off days before the city's earliest foundations were
laid as a French fur-traders' outpost. The "Golden Boy" above the
dome holds a torch in one hand – and in the other a sheaf of wheat.*

Lower Fort Gary, about 32 kilometres (20 miles) north of
Winnipeg, was built by the Hudson's Bay Company between 1831
and 1847. As late as 1911 it was still an important trading post for
the company. The governor's stone house stands within the fort.
Among the displays are a fine collection of Indian relics, the fur loft,
a York boat and a Red River cart.

Manitoba has a diverse cultural heritage. At Steinbach a pioneer village depicts the life of the first Mennonites, who came here from Russia seeking religious freedom in 1874. Mennonites are noted for their tasty and hearty fare, like "shoofly pie", which is so good you have to "shoo" the flies away, and chicken-pot pie. Such food is served at the village.

There are two groups of Mennonites in Canada: the Russian Mennonites of Manitoba and the Pennsylvania-Dutch of Ontario. In the seventeenth century they fled from Europe, some to Russia and some to the United States. Many moved on, the former to Manitoba to escape persecution, and the latter to Ontario to remain under the English Crown following the American War of Independence.

Central Canada

"Then it was that a third voice, mightier than the others, lifted itself up in the silence: the voice of Quebec. . . . It came to her with the sound of a church bell, with the majesty of an organ's tones, like a plaintive love-song, like the long high call of woodsmen in the forest. For verily there was in it all that makes the soul of the Province: the loved solemnities of the ancestral faith; the lilt of that old speech guarded with jealous care; the grandeur and the barbaric strength of this new land where an ancient race has again found its youth."

Louis Hémon, author

"Rivers define the character of every land through which they flow and in Ontario they are witnesses to the schizophrenic geography of our richest, most populous, and second-largest province. The gentle streams of the settled south remind you of English shires and the broad valleys of central Germany. But to find anything resembling the rivers of the Ontarian north you would have to go to Lapland or Siberia."

Hugh MacLennan, author

A farm at Tewkesbury in la belle province.

Sun breaks through the freezing mist at Hornepayne, Ontario – a railway town about 161 kilometres (100 miles) north of Michipicoten. In such towns the railway is still the lifeline – as it once was throughout most of Canada – particularly during the long and bitter winters. In the summer there is a different toll to pay for the privilege of living in this largely unspoiled area – contending with a voracious population of mosquitoes and blackflies.

Michipicoten Harbour is on Lake Superior, the deepest and largest of the Great Lakes — it is 616 kilometres (383 miles) long. Thunder Bay, at the head of the Great Lakes, is the third largest Canadian port for ocean-going vessels and the main port for transshipment of golden prairie wheat. The Great Lakes system is one of the most important natural features of the North American continent. The combined area of the lakes is the largest surface of fresh water in the world. To the west of Lake Superior is Quetico Provincial Park, a wilderness teeming with wildlife. To the far north on Hudson Bay is Ontario's immense Polar Bear Provincial Park, where bears, caribou, arctic foxes and snow geese live undisturbed.

Above: *The icy splendour of winter fishing from an Ontario dam.
Once a necessity, fishing is now a pleasure for tens of thousands of
fishermen drawn by the special appeal which this sport offers. This
determined individual perfectly sums up the romance — and the
anguish — of the sport.*

Right: *At the "Soo" Locks at Sault Ste Marie, Ontario, visitors
can view the world's largest locks, which are situated between Lake
Huron and Lake Superior, from special observation towers.
Because of its prime location, Sault Ste Marie has a number of
industries, including steel-making.*

Top: Sainte-Marie among the Hurons is a reconstructed Jesuit Mission at Midland, Ontario where students in costume act as guides.

Above: Strange limestone formations resembling huge flower pots adorn Flower Pot Island, one of the fifty that comprise Georgian Bay Islands National Park.

The International Nickel Company of Canada (INCO)
superstack rises above a barren landscape. Ontario has a wealth of
natural resources, nickel being one of the most important. At
Sudbury INCO mines most of the world's nickel. The
devastated land is now being renewed. Groups of young people and
others scatter limestone to neutralize the soil, and greenery is
beginning to sprout again.

Sap is collected from maple sugar trees at Weber's Sugar Bush near Elmira, Ontario. The Indians first taught the settlers in Ontario and Quebec how to tap the trees for the sap and to boil it for the incomparable resulting treats – maple sugar and maple syrup. The Mennonites who settled the Kitchener-Waterloo area are famed for their beautifully kept farms and for a life style that excludes modern amenities. At the wonderful Mennonite market held each Saturday near Kitchener, there are home-made sausages, freshly baked pies and colourfully patterned quilts.

Above: *Dundalk, Ontario, and the Kimberley Ski Area just north of Dundalk, are at a slightly higher altitude than the surrounding land, which creates a localized snow belt. But each summer there is time to take a break from farm work for Dundalk's Square and Step-Dancing Competition. Shelburne, a few kilometres to the south-east, has an annual Fiddlers' Contest, and Flesherton, to the north of Dundalk, has a Split-Rail Festival every September.*

Left: *Ontario's provincial flower – the trillium – has for many years been a protected species.*

77

Left: *The Steel City – Hamilton, Ontario – on the western tip of Lake Ontario, is also famed for its large – 809 hectares (2000 acres) – and long-established Royal Botanical Gardens. More recently, the city has acquired a marvellous new cultural centre, Hamilton Place.*

Above: *The Niagara Peninsula, Ontario's main fruit-growing area, is especially delightful at blossom-time. The "fruit belt" is protected on one side by the Niagara Escarpment, seen in the distance, and is under the moderating influence of Lake Ontario on the other side. The area, with such centres as Grimsby, Beamsville, Vineland and Jordan, produces tonnes of grapes, peaches, apples, cherries, pears and plums. The soil is particularly well suited to grapes just above the escarpment. Vineyards, the largest in Canada, have been established here since 1812.*

The Eaton Centre in Toronto is a supreme example of Canadian merchandizing. Timothy Eaton's motto "Goods satisfactory or money refunded" has appealed to generations of customers. In this sophisticated new shopping complex, the glass archway, blocks long, and tinted with pale colours, hints at its European inspiration – Milan's Galleria Victor Emmanuel.

Casa Loma, Toronto, was the fairy-tale castle of Sir Henry and Lady Pellatt. This extraordinary structure cost the eccentric and extremely rich stockbroker $3 million. It was built between 1911 and 1914 in a fascinating conglomeration of styles that appealed to Sir Henry – from Norman and Gothic to Elizabethan and Edwardian. Casa Loma had gold-plated faucets in the bathrooms, one of the largest wine cellars in North America, and a library to hold 100 000 volumes. This attempt at living like royalty failed, due to the enormous rise in costs after the First World War. The castle was eventually taken over by the Kiwanis Club of West Toronto, who run it as a tourist attraction and raise large sums of money for charity.

*In the summer students from Queen's University man the cannon
at Old Fort Henry, Kingston. The fort, unusually, faces inland.
It was intended to guard the land approach to Point Frederick
where there was a naval dockyard. Queen's, one of Canada's oldest
and most distinguished universities, was founded in 1841. More than
10000 students undertake a diversity of studies from Arts and
Science and Applied Science to Law and Medicine.*

An international bridge connects Prescott, Ontario, and Ogdensburg, New York. The St Lawrence is indisputably one of the great waterways of the world – a mighty 1207-kilometre (750-mile) river which cannot be intimidated by the huge ships that use it. Since the opening in 1959 of the St Lawrence Seaway, a great engineering feat which was a joint Canadian-United States venture, 3768 kilometres (2341 miles) of waterways for deep-draft ocean-going vessels have been opened up, and a total of 15 286 kilometres (9499 miles) of navigable waterways for smaller ships and boats.

Overleaf: *At Upper Canada Village, near Morrisburg, Ontario, on the St Lawrence, the sights and sounds of the late eighteenth and early nineteenth centuries are re-created.*

Another Expo feature remains, the "Habitat" apartments (above), *providing much desired accommodation by the water. The city's administration has brought to Montreal other global events, perhaps most memorably the 1976 Summer Olympics.*

Right: *The heavenly blues of the interior of the Gothic-Revival-style Notre Dame Church, Montreal – only one of the many Roman Catholic churches and institutions in the city. In fact the city was founded as a mission for the Indians.*

A convivial community of ice-fishing huts – perhaps as many as 15000 – stands on the solidly frozen Sainte-Anne River close to La Pérade, near the St Lawrence. Ensconced in his warm and cosy hut, complete with furniture, refreshments and maybe even a television set, the fisherman casts his line for tommycod or le petit poisson des cheneaux. *Every January ice-fishing begins again, and the general merriment, singing and dancing continues night and day for up to seven weeks. Where else does such* joie de vivre *accompany this usually sedate activity?*

The Plains of Abraham, Quebec, where in 1759 General Wolfe
and the Marquis de Montcalm fell, are in Battlefield Park, the
city's largest park, which extends from the city's boundaries to the
walls of the dramatically situated Citadelle. With good reason
Quebec was sometimes called "the Gibraltar of America". The
narrowing of the river and the sheer heights combined to make this a
battlefield that was to change the course of Canada's history.
This was not the end of Quebec's history as a battleground. A few
years later, at the beginning of the American Revolution, troops
were sent here by the Thirteen Colonies to persuade the Québeçois to
join the Revolution. The troops and Benedict Arnold were repulsed.

Left: *The pure fantasy of a castle built entirely of ice captures the spirit of the ten-day-long Bonhomme Carnaval, the Québeçois version of Mardi Gras. Fortified against cold by an anti-freeze for humans called "Cariboo", citizens and visitors enjoy parades, costume balls, snow-sculpture contests, dancing in the streets and the Canoe Race – where superbly trained crews row and pull their boats over the drifting ice and freezing water of the St Lawrence. This is Quebec's exuberant affirmation of life in the face of a crushingly cold winter and provides a welcome prelude to the restraints of the following Lenten period.*

More than ninety per cent of the people of Quebec are of French ancestry and are determinedly proud of the past and of their cultural life. Visitors wandering through the streets of Vieux Québec can enjoy fine food and music (below) and feast their eyes on the architecture of Old France. The city has always charmed those seeing it for the first time. In 1842, when Charles Dickens visited the city, he was enchanted.

Quebec, its Château Frontenac (above) *high above the Lower Town, encapsulates the spirit of French Canada. Over a million visitors a year succumb to the grace and beauty of the oldest city in Canada and North America's most European. The Upper Town, built on the heights of Cape Diamond, is the centre of cultural and artistic life in the city. From the Dufferin Terrace in front of the Château, one can rent a horsedrawn calèche, or simply stand and admire the spectacular views of the river, the Ile d'Orléans, which here divides the St Lawrence in two, and the heights of Lévis on the south shore beyond. Pedestrians can enjoy the view from the stairs* (right) *which link the Upper and Lower Towns.*

Atlantic Canada

"Maritimers are a seafaring race whose roots are deep in history .... A sense of history clings about the silvery weathered shingles of fishermen's huts; the vivid colours of boats and lobster floats – red, blue, ochre, green – and the black-and-white dazzle of painted wooden houses are affirmations of life and vigour against the hard grey weather and the dangerous ocean. Men have been here a long time; they have come to terms with the forests, the rocks, the tides."

Kildare Dobbs, writer and broadcaster

"Newfoundland is of the sea. Poised like a mighty granite stopper over the bell-mouth of the Gulf of St Lawrence, it turns its back upon the greater continent barricading itself behind the three-hundred-mile-long rampart that forms its hostile western coast. Its other coasts all face toward the open ocean, and are so slashed and convoluted with bays, inlets, runs, and fjords that they offer more than five thousand miles of shoreline to the sweep of the Atlantic."

Farley Mowat, author

The Cabot Trail, Cape Breton Island, Nova Scotia, takes visitors past impressive seascapes.

Saint John, New Brunswick, a deep-water port and railway terminus, is also famous for its Reversing Falls Rapids, shown here. Tourists like to marvel at the swift reverse currents, which flow up the Saint John River during tides as high as 21 metres (70 feet) in the Bay of Fundy, where the world's highest tides occur.

*Fall leaves frame the Shogomoc River near where it joins the
Saint John River at Meductic. Chilly nights and warm days, with
no sudden cold snaps, ensure a brilliant display of scarlet and gold.
And the mysterious and powerful scents of fall excite the blood –
a prelude to the wintery blasts ahead.*

Prince Edward Island National Park (below) *is on the north shore of the island, a tiny crescent set in sparkling waters on Canada's massive tapestry. Its 1609 kilometres (1000 miles) of pink sandy beaches frame the red sandy loam. This rich earth ensures the success of the patchwork of farms. The Indians called the island* Abegweit, *meaning "cradled in the waves", and it is thought that they cultivated the land for untold summers before their world was shattered. On his first voyage in 1534, Jacques Cartier described the island as "the fairest one could possible see" and ". . . full of pease, white and red gooseberries, strawberries, raspberries and wild wheat like rye, which looks as if it had been sowed and cultivated".*

Above: *Massive rocks and a prim but sturdy lighthouse near Peggy's Cove, Nova Scotia watch over the land when the sea threatens. Two ferries cross Northumberland Strait, one between Prince Edward Island and Nova Scotia, and the other between Prince Edward Island and New Brunswick – comforting links with the mainland.*

Citadel Hill, Halifax, is one of Nova Scotia's most important historic sites. The Citadel was Britain's answer to the French Fortress of Louisbourg (pages 124-125) in the fierce tit-for-tat power struggles of the seventeenth century. Halifax is many things to a Nova Scotian – capital, university town, cultural centre and port.

Peggy's Cove, Nova Scotia, is everyone's idea of what a fishing village should look like. Suitably picturesque for artists and tourists alike, it has attracted both for many, many years. In fact, a number of artists choose to reside in this province, Peggy's Cove, Mahone Bay and Lunenburg (page 125) being particularly favoured.

Above: *Cheerfully attired in the simple, clear colours of a folk-art painting, Lunenburg, Nova Scotia, is strongly reminiscent of its German Mennonite founders. Nova Scotia has welcomed many other peoples as well. Where else could you find a French fortress, a Gaelic college (St Anne's) complete with a Gathering of the Clans, and a "Mennonite" fishing village with the world's most advanced fish-processing plant?*

Left: *Spring comes to the Fortress of Louisbourg near the eastern tip of Cape Breton Island. The meticulously reconstructed Fortress is the magnificent focal point of a 6070-hectare (15000-acre) National Historic Park. Built by the French, Louisbourg was a seemingly indestructible symbol of the struggles and instabilities that Maritimers endured for centuries. So powerful a symbol was it, that ultimately it was torn apart, stone by stone. Today, hundreds of thousands of visitors are drawn to this memorable site. The journey is made easier by a causeway, built in 1955, which has riveted Cape Breton Island to the rest of Nova Scotia once and for all.*

Above: *Boats and lobster traps lie beached at St George's Bay,*
Port au Port Peninsula, in south-western Newfoundland.
Newfoundlanders are never far from the sea or from their fishing
gear. Skills carefully honed by centuries of struggle and hardship
remain strong and vital.
The rugged sea-smashed coastline is dotted with fishing villages.
Isolation nurtures the telling of stories and the singing of sea-
shanties. Now, people are moving towards centres like St John's
(right) *where fishing vessels have anchored for half a millennium.*
The colours of the frame houses seem to say that summer is short,
but it is here; winter is hard, but it will end; so tell us a story, sing
us a song.

Harp seals winter off Newfoundland, where the pups are
born on the ice floes. Pure white at birth, they undergo a series of
colour changes, becoming for a time a mottled dark grey. When
fully adult a harp- or horseshoe-shaped band will appear on their
backs. Labrador, two-thirds of the total land area of
Newfoundland, is almost uninhabited – a white paradise for
Arctic wildlife.
Ice floes and icebergs sometimes threaten the North Atlantic
shipping lanes. Recent oil exploration off the coasts is dangerous
work, made much more perilous here by these enormous and
unpredictable masses of ice.